The purchase of this book was made

possible by a grant from the

Weller Foundation

GROUNDBREAKERS

Edwin Hubble

Fiona Macdonald

Heinemann Library
Chicago, Illinois

FE 26 '02

Visit our website at www.heinemannlibrary.com

Designed by Katrina ffiske
Illustrated by Michael Posen
Originated by Ambassador Litho
Printed in Hong Kong

05 04 03 02 01
10 9 8 7 6 5 4 3 2 1

Library of Congress Cataloging-in-Publication Data
Macdonald, Fiona.
   Edwin Hubble / Fiona Macdonald.
     p. cm. -- (Groundbreakers; 2)
   Includes bibliographical references and index.
   ISBN 1-58810-054-5 (library)
   1. Hubble, Edwin Powell, 1889-1953--Juvenile literature. 2. Astronomers--United
States--Biography--Juvenile literature. [1. Hubble, Edwin Powell, 1889-1953. 2.
Astronomers.] I. Title. II. Series.

   QB36.H83 M33 2001
   520'.92--dc21
   [B]
               37777002086262   00-063266

Acknowledgments
The author and publishers are grateful to the following for permission to reproduce copyright material: AKG London, pp. 7, 17, 21, 31; Art Archive p. 33; National Archives, p. 34; Corbis, p. 9; Robert Holmes, pp. 13, 37; Roger Ressmeyer/ Henry E. Huntington Library and Art Gallery, pp. 5, 8, 16, 20, 22, 23, 28, 30, 38, 39; Hulton Getty, pp. 11, 18; Mary Evans Picture Library, pp. 10, 12; MPM Images, pp. 15, 25, 41, 43; Popperfoto, p. 36; Science and Society Picture Library, p. 32; Associated Press, p. 42; Science Photo Library/NASA, pp. 4, 14; Peter Bassett, pp. 19, 24, 26; Harvard College Observatory, p. 27; Space Telescope Science Institute/NASA, pp. 29, 40; Martin Bond, A. Sharov & I. Novikov, p. 6.

Cover photograph reproduced with the permission of Henry E. Huntington Library and Art Gallery.

Some words are shown in bold, **like this.** You can find out what they mean by looking in the glossary.

Contents

Exploring the Universe 4

Early Years 6

The Young Man 8

Across the Atlantic 10

Back Home 12

Studying Astronomy 14

War Hero? 16

Mount Wilson 18

Constant Companions 20

Observing the Stars 22

The "Great Debate" 24

A Great Discovery 26

The Expanding Universe 28

The High Life 30

Back to War 32

Problems at Home 34

Seeing Farther into Space 36

Illness and Disappointment 38

After Hubble 40

Hubble's Memorial 42

Timeline 44

More Books to Read 45

Glossary 46

Index 48

Exploring the Universe

Edwin Hubble looked relaxed and confident outside Mount Wilson Observatory in 1924. He was 35 years old when this photo was taken.

Born in 1889, American **astronomer** Edwin Hubble is remembered today as the man who searched "for the boundaries of the universe." His work still guides astronomers today.

One universe, or more?

A brilliant observer of the night sky, Hubble spent almost all his working life at Mount Wilson **Observatory** in California. He used the Mount Wilson telescope to investigate **nebulae,** mysterious, cloudy objects in space, and **galaxies,** collections of stars held together by **gravity.** Hubble worked out a way of measuring how far nebulae and other objects were from Earth. Then he used this information to solve a problem that had been puzzling astronomers for many years—is our galaxy, the **Milky Way,** equal to the whole universe, or are there millions of other galaxies scattered throughout space? In a stunning piece of scientific thinking, he proved that there is only one universe, but that it contains billions of other galaxies. Our galaxy is just a tiny part of an enormous universe.

Hubble also noticed that galaxies could be grouped according to their shapes. He created a classification system that astronomers still use today to help them identify different types of galaxies.

An expanding universe

Hubble's greatest achievement is that he was the first person to find real evidence that the universe is expanding. The nebulae and galaxies he saw through the telescope were moving away from Earth and from each other. Linked to this discovery, he devised the **Hubble constant,** a form of mathematical shorthand, to help astronomers measure the rate at which the universe is growing, and to calculate its age. Hubble's groundbreaking discoveries have transformed our understanding of the universe, suggesting how it might have been created and how it might end.

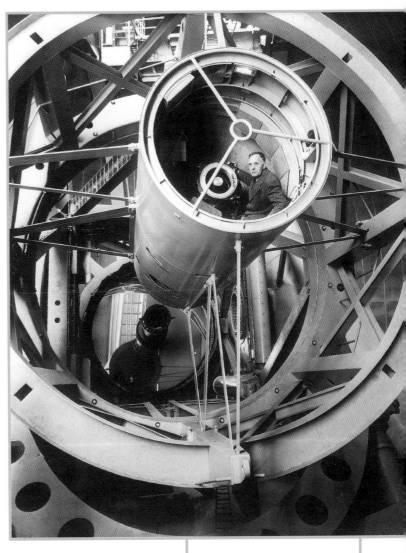

Hubble sits at the controls of the massive Hale telescope at Mount Palomar Observatory in California.

ONGOING IMPACT   Hubble Space Telescope

Today, Hubble's name has become well known to many people who are not scientists or astronomers. They have been amazed, impressed, and sometimes deeply moved by the magnificent photos beamed back to Earth by the Hubble Space Telescope (HST), which was named in Hubble's honor and launched in 1990.

Early Years

Edwin Powell Hubble was born on November 20, 1889, in Marshfield, Missouri, where his grandparents owned a farm. He was the third of eight children, three boys and five girls. Edwin's family was not rich, but it was well respected in Marshfield. His parents had many distinguished ancestors, including local politicians and soldiers who had fought in the Civil War.

Edwin's father, John, was an insurance salesman. This meant that he was often away on business. John never seemed very close to his children, even when he was at home. He was strict and insisted on good behavior at all times. Edwin's mother, Virginia Lee, known as Jennie, was a very different character—warm, loving, and calm. The Hubbles' lifestyle was very plain and simple.

Both of Edwin's parents were deeply religious and regularly attended their local Baptist church. As a boy, Edwin helped with Sunday school classes and sang in the church choir.

Marshfield was a typical American country town—small, quiet, rather sleepy, yet proud of its local traditions.

Edwin (third from the right) posed with some of his brothers, sisters, and cousins outside their grandparents' home.

First sight of the stars

Edwin liked the outdoor life of the farm. He became very fond of animals, was a good ice-skater, and enjoyed hiking and fishing. The wide skies above Missouri also gave him his first glimpse of the stars. His grandfather was interested in stargazing and kept a large telescope in the garden. When Edwin was eight years old, his grandfather allowed him to stay up late to look through the telescope as a birthday treat. Edwin remained fascinated by **astronomy** for the rest of his life.

Chicago was a busy, wealthy city when the Hubble family moved to Wheaton. Many people were moving to the city, hoping to get rich.

A NEW HOME

In 1901, Edwin's family moved to Wheaton, a new town close to Chicago—the major city in the Midwest. Chicago's wealth came from trade. Thousands of trains carried cattle and corn from midwestern farms and western ranches to Chicago factories, where they were processed and sent to customers living in cities on the east coast. Downtown, there were offices and shops, together with a fine new university—where Edwin would later study—and some of the world's first skyscrapers, such as the Home Insurance Building, built in 1885.

7

The Young Man

Edwin (center, back row) posed with other student athletes from the University of Chicago in 1907.

Edwin was a bright student. He was almost always in the top ten in his class, and his best subjects were English, math, history, and Latin. His one weak point was spelling, which he never completely mastered. His letters remained full of mistakes for his whole life!

Edwin also excelled at sports. From his early teenage years, he was one of the tallest boys in the school. He was strong and full of energy. He played for the school basketball and football teams, and took part in athletic contests. The high jump and pole vault were some of his specialties. Success at sports made him popular with his schoolmates and in the local community.

However, Edwin's behavior was not as remarkable. His mother worried because he seemed distant and secretive, like his father, and kept his feelings to himself. His teachers complained that he was uncooperative in class, and that he talked back to them, or interrupted classes with rude remarks. This may have been because he was bored. A school friend remembered that Edwin was always very quick to finish his work.

JAMES KEELER

As a young student, Hubble was excited by seeing the famous Halley's Comet, which was visible from Earth in 1910. Around this time, American **astronomers** such as James Keeler (1850–1900) were making important steps forward in studying stars. Keeler took some of the best-yet photographs of mysterious, cloudy objects in the sky, called **nebulae.** Years later, nebulae were to be the main subject of Hubble's own research.

A burning ambition

Edwin started school in Wheaton when he was almost twelve. The town had a small **observatory,** with a telescope for studying the stars. There is no record of him using it, but from his letters to his grandfather back in Marshfield, we know that Edwin was still very interested in **astronomy.** In 1906, Edwin left school and enrolled at the University of Chicago. He wanted to study astronomy, but his father would not allow it. He hoped that Edwin would train to be a lawyer instead. To please his father, Edwin agreed to study law, languages, and **philosophy,** but he also took classes in math, physics, and astronomy.

Although obviously clever, Edwin did not seem outstanding to his family or friends. But one teacher spotted his potential, saying:

"Edwin Hubble will be one of the most brilliant men of his generation."

(From *Edwin Hubble, Mariner of the Nebulae* by Gale E. Christianson)

University life

Edwin enjoyed student life. He lived at the university, in a residence hall with other young men. Their main amusements were singing and putting on plays. Edwin had a good voice and enjoyed acting. No longer bored and restless, he became more outgoing, and was popular with the other students. Edwin was also asked to play for some university sports teams, but his father banned him from football, saying it was too dangerous. Edwin secretly took up boxing instead! He turned out to be a talented boxer, and became a local champion.

The University of Chicago, where Edwin studied, was founded in 1890. Some of the best scholars in the United States were employed as teachers and researchers there.

Across the Atlantic

This view looks across the roofs of several college buildings at the University of Oxford, in England. Edwin fell in love with the city's ancient buildings and "dreaming spires."

(ONGOING IMPACT) Studying nebulae

While Edwin was at Oxford, one special question fascinated United States astronomers: what were **nebulae?** Some, like James Keeler of Lick **Observatory,** California, thought they were new planets being made. Others thought they might be distant collections of stars, but until a new telescope was built in 1912 at the Lowell Observatory in Arizona, they had no way of taking good enough photographs to test their ideas. From 1912 on, many of the United States's greatest astronomers, including Vesto Slipher and Harlow Shapley, studied nebulae. Before long, they would be joined by Edwin Hubble himself.

During his third year at the University of Chicago, Edwin decided to apply for a Rhodes **scholarship.** This was a prize awarded to just two students from each state in the country. It paid for them to travel across the Atlantic and spend three years studying at a British university. It also gave them the chance to explore Europe during their vacations and to become familiar with European culture. Competition for these scholarships was as fierce then as it is today. Students had to take a very difficult exam, go through interviews, and provide references from teachers and community leaders. But Edwin succeeded.

In September 1910, Edwin left Chicago and began his studies at Oxford—the oldest, and one of the most famous, universities in Britain.

Making time to study

Still aiming to please his father, Edwin agreed to study law. But he decided to squeeze all his law studies into just two years, so that he would have time to take courses in other subjects that interested him more during his final year. This meant doing a great deal of work in a very short time, but Edwin managed it, and got good grades as well. He also kept up his interest in **astronomy.** In one of his letters home, he proudly told his family how he had corrected some Oxford science students, who had misunderstood important new research by a United States **astronomer.**

Members of the Oxford and Cambridge University boat crews posed for this photograph in about 1900–10 with their dog mascots.

A British way of life

Edwin did not spend all his Oxford time studying. He made friends with many wealthy British students, and liked the life they introduced him to. With his new friends, he enjoyed parties, dinners, concerts, and going to the theater, and was invited for weekend visits to grand country houses. He also played sports and went on bicycling trips with other students. One summer, they pedaled 1,000 miles (1,600 kilometers) across Europe. Edwin's skill at foreign languages was very useful on these travels.

BRITISH STYLE

During his time at Oxford, Edwin became a great admirer of all things British. He praised British books, plays, gardens, and stately homes. He wore British-style tweed jackets and "plus fours," or baggy calf-length trousers. He even began to speak with a British accent. Edwin kept his love of British style, and traces of the accent, for the rest of his life.

Back Home

R.M.S. Mauretania

Edwin crossed the Atlantic in a steam-powered ship like this one. These boats were called ocean liners. Traveling on them took a long time.

LONG DISTANCE

In 1913, when Edwin's father died, the only way of sending messages across the Atlantic Ocean was by letter, carried on board ships. There were no transatlantic telephone cables, and planes had not yet managed to fly that far. The only way of traveling between Europe and the United States was by sea. The crossing took almost a week, and had to be booked a long time in advance.

Before Edwin had finished his studies at Oxford, his father became ill and died. The slow speed of travel at that time made it impossible for Edwin to go back home for his father's funeral. But he cut short his plans to spend a third summer in Europe and hurried home to the United States as soon as his final term at Oxford was over. By this time, his family had moved to Louisville, Kentucky.

Money worries

Edwin's father's death had left the family with financial problems. His older brother was ill and had not been able to get the family out of debt. As the oldest capable son, Edwin felt that it was his duty to take responsibility for the whole family. He promised to stay with his mother for a whole year, until she felt able to manage alone. Edwin's mother was very pleased to have him back home again, but he turned out not to be much help, leading the family even further into debt. It was Edwin's younger brother, William, called Bill, who saved the family's fortunes.

Bill left college to find work. He decided never to marry, but to send all the money he could spare to his mother and sisters.

The end of his dreams?

Humbled and perhaps slightly ashamed, Edwin found part-time work as a teacher. His subjects included physics and Spanish. He also worked as a legal clerk. He still hoped to pass his professional law exams, although he never ended up taking them. Edwin's pupils later remembered him as fun and slightly eccentric—he wore European-style cloaks and plus-fours to school. However, he had little patience and was not very good at explaining difficult topics to young students.

The year 1913–14 was a low point in Edwin's career. After his academic success at Chicago and his interesting, enjoyable years at Oxford, he was back in small-town America, poorly paid, and doing work he did not enjoy. But he had not forgotten his ambition to be an **astronomer.** After keeping his promise to his mother to spend a year with her, Edwin decided it was time for a change.

These high school students are shown studying physics in 1915. Edwin Hubble would have taught in a school much like this one.

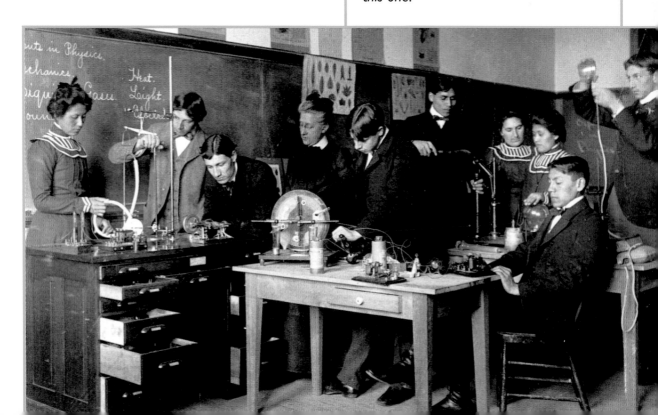

Studying Astronomy

Yerkes Observatory in Wisconsin was where Edwin learned how to make scientific observations of the stars. The observatory had the biggest telescope in the world for twelve years. Edwin worked on it.

In late summer 1914, Edwin went back to the University of Chicago. This time, there was no question of studying law—he was determined to be an **astronomer.** The professor who had taught Edwin science when he had been a student there remembered him well and decided to help him. Edwin needed money for food, rent, and university fees. But there were no grants, and it was too late to apply for a **scholarship.** So the professor recommended him for a job at the nearby Yerkes **Observatory** at Williams Bay, Wisconsin—a research station housing a large telescope used for studying the stars. It was the perfect part-time job.

Learning all the time

Edwin arrived at Yerkes Observatory in August 1914. He worked as an assistant to the senior astronomers there, helping them to operate the huge telescope, take photographs of the night sky, and record their results. All the time, he was learning useful skills that he would employ for the rest of his life. He also attended lectures and classes at the University of Chicago and began a research project of his own.

Studying nebulae

Edwin chose to study **nebulae.** These mysterious objects in space had puzzled astronomers for hundreds of years. In 1914, the leading expert on nebulae was Vesto Slipher, of Lowell Observatory, near Flagstaff, Arizona. He had spent the past ten years photographing them, and now was ready to announce his findings. Edwin was present at the scientific meeting where Slipher revealed his astonishing discovery: nebulae are actually moving, very quickly, away from the sun.

For the next two years, Edwin scanned the skies with the Yerkes telescope to find nebulae. He photographed them, measured their brightness and size, identified them in **star atlases** or noted them as new discoveries, and recorded how fast they were moving through space. All this work produced no startling results at the time, but it provided extra knowledge that would be useful to him later. Edwin worked so hard that in 1916, he was offered a full-time job as an astronomer at the famous Mount Wilson Observatory, near Pasadena in California.

*The Andromeda nebula is 2.3 million **light-years** away from Earth. Edwin chose to study nebulae at the university.*

DIFFERENT KINDS OF NEBULAE

Today, thanks to Hubble and other astronomers, we know that there are several different kinds of nebulae. Some are clouds of high energy gas around newly forming stars; some are "shells" of glowing gas surrounding decaying stars; some are dark clouds of space dust and gas that block light from stars behind them; some are clouds of dust that shine with reflected starlight; and some are actual **galaxies.**

War Hero?

Edwin poses in his U.S. Army uniform, around 1918. His sister Lucy is next to him, dressed in her nurse's uniform.

In 1914, just as Edwin was starting work at Yerkes **Observatory,** World War I broke out. Almost all the nations of Europe were involved, **allied** either with Germany, on one side, or with Britain and France on the other. At first, everyone expected that the war would be over by Christmas 1914, but it dragged on for four long years. Toward the end of the war, the United States also became involved, on the British side.

Helping his friends

Edwin was deeply distressed when the war began. He knew that many of the students he had met in Oxford and on his travels in Europe would be involved in the fighting, and that many of them would be killed, especially once the war began to claim huge numbers of soldiers' lives. When the United States entered the war in 1917, Edwin volunteered to join the army and fight to defend Britain. His sister Lucy also volunteered, and served as a Red Cross nurse.

Army life

The U.S. Army welcomed men like Edwin, who were intelligent, healthy, brave, and strong. He was made an officer almost as soon as he joined. At first, he was sent to army camps in the U.S., where he helped to train other recruits. Here, he proved his endurance on long marches in bitter winter weather. He also demonstrated his excellent hand-eye coordination—that is, how well he could use his hands and eyes together—by defeating a high-ranking officer at target-shooting. In the past, this coordination had helped him win at sports. In the future, it would make him an expert at handling huge, complicated telescopes.

In 1918, Edwin traveled to France with the U.S. Army. He was fully prepared to risk his life on the battlefield, but was never involved in any serious action. His unit arrived in Europe right at the end of the war and was not needed for fighting. But Edwin proved himself to be a good officer. He was promoted, and ended the war with the rank of major.

WORLD WAR I

Some people would call Edwin's decision to join the army noble or heroic. As an American, there was no need for him to take part in the war. By 1917, he knew that millions of young European men had been killed—or very seriously injured—as they fought in awful conditions on the front lines, in Belgium and northern France. There, enemy armies came face to face in a sea of mud, shell craters, and barbed wire.

Many towns and cities were badly damaged by fighting during World War I. This ruined street is in France, where Edwin went with the U.S. Army.

Mount Wilson

LIGHT TELESCOPES

Light telescopes, such as the one Hubble used at Mount Wilson, work by collecting light rays from distant objects, and passing them through lenses or reflecting them with mirrors to produce a magnified image. The larger the telescope, the farther it can "see." Telescopes for studying the stars are usually built on remote mountaintops, where the air is pure and clear, far away from the bright lights of houses and cars.

Edwin returned to the U.S. in 1919. Stopping in Chicago for only one day to meet his mother and sisters, he headed straight for Pasadena, California, to take up the post at Mount Wilson **Observatory** that he had been offered in 1916. The main telescope at Mount Wilson and the **astronomers** who used it were world famous. Edwin felt proud to be part of such a team. He also felt ambitious. At last he had the chance to make a name for himself.

Working all night

Edwin's exhausting task at Mount Wilson was to share in a regular routine of night-time observations.

The dome of Mount Wilson Observatory in Pasadena housed the largest telescope in the world. Edwin made his most important discoveries here.

Annie Jump Cannon's work helped other astronomers with their observations.

Setting and handling the huge telescope called for great skill and attention to detail, and each observation could take several hours to complete. The best nights for observing were bright and frosty, with no clouds. This meant that the vast hall housing the telescope was often extremely cold. Unless astronomers were careful, their tears froze and their eyelashes stuck to the viewfinder. Edwin found his army greatcoat very useful for keeping warm. He also liked to wear his old army clothes and polished leather boots. At first, his colleagues found this rather strange—they were also surprised by his slight British accent—but they soon came to respect Edwin's intelligence and admire the quality of his work.

The "monastery"

Although there were many expert women astronomers in the United States at the time, including Henrietta Leavitt and Annie Jump Cannon, only men were allowed to work at Mount Wilson, apart from a female housekeeper and a cook. The male astronomers made a joke of this, calling the building where they slept in between spells of observations "the monastery." Life there was very simple, with narrow beds, hard chairs, and plain food, but Edwin enjoyed it.

Constant Companions

Grace Burke (1899–1981) married Edwin in 1924, and remained his closest companion for the rest of his life.

In 1920, less than a year after Edwin arrived in California, he met the woman who was to change his life. Her name was Grace Burke, and she had come with a group of friends to visit the Mount Wilson **Observatory.** A trip to Mount Wilson was a popular outing for many Californians at the time. Visitors came for the dramatic drive through spectacular mountain scenery, and to gaze in awe at the huge dome that covered the great telescope. Important visitors—or friends of the **astronomers** who worked there—were given a special guided tour, and met the staff on duty. Edwin was working at Mount Wilson on the day that Grace was shown around.

A good-looking man

We do not know what Edwin thought of their first meeting, but Grace seems to have been very impressed. Many people who met Edwin commented on his appearance. His height was striking—he was over six feet tall, and he had a fine, muscular physique. His face also fit the "film star" image of the time, with strong, clean-cut features, neatly trimmed hair, and clear hazel eyes.

California girl

Photographs show Grace as petite, dark-haired, and stylishly dressed. Grace and Edwin had a lot in common. She was intelligent, and had been to Stanford University, where she had studied literature and languages. She also enjoyed art, sports, and the countryside. But unlike Edwin, Grace came from a very privileged background. Her family was wealthy, well known, and at the top of Californian society. Grace liked to mix with other rich and talented people.

Grace was married when she first met Edwin, but her husband, a mining engineer, died in a mining accident the following year. Grace and Edwin became very close, and eventually married in 1924. For the rest of their lives, they were devoted companions. They spent as much time together as they could, planning and furnishing a lovely new home, or leaving the city to enjoy fishing and hiking trips in the countryside. They had no children, but loved their several pet cats. Like many other women at that time, Grace saw it as her life's work to support her husband. She believed that he would one day be a great man, and that it was her duty to help him in any way she could.

Grace would have been dressed like these wealthy, fashionable young women of the 1920s when she met Edwin.

Observing the Stars

The Mount Wilson telescope could see farther and more clearly into space than any other telescope on Earth. It was also fitted with very sensitive cameras. Working night after night, Edwin and his colleagues used these cameras to take huge photographs of distant stars, so that they could study them later on. By looking at hundreds of photographs collected over long periods of time, the **astronomers** could spot changes in known stars, or find new ones. The telescope and its cameras also helped them to discover many new space objects they had been unable to see before.

Quarrels

Throughout his career as an astronomer, Edwin was particularly interested in **nebulae.** Following his research at Yerkes **Observatory,** he used the powerful Mount Wilson telescope to collect as much new information about these mysterious "star-clouds" as possible. His studies fit neatly with many of the topics researched by his colleagues at Mount Wilson—although he did not always agree with their ideas. He also did not like some of them, and this often made his life at Mount Wilson very awkward indeed.

*This photograph shows the Mount Wilson telescope. Its main mirror was 100 inches (254 centimeters) wide and weighed over 5 tons. At the bottom of the picture, through the railings, is the chair where Edwin Hubble sat and observed objects over a million **light-years** away from Earth.*

Edwin is at the middle in the back row of this picture of the observatory staff, standing beside a man with very white hair. Van Maanen is in the front row, second from left.

Two of Edwin's least favorite colleagues were Harlow Shapley and a Dutchman, Adriaan van Maanen. They were talented astronomers who used photos from the Mount Wilson telescope to try and answer the most important astronomical questions of the day. Like Edwin, Shapley had been born in small-town Missouri, to a family without much money. But unlike Edwin, Shapley was not ashamed of his roots, and never tried to hide them. Van Maanen was loud, cheerful, and fond of silly jokes. Both men mocked Edwin, with his British accent and British clothes.

PHOTOGRAPHING STARS

The first star photo, of our nearest star—the sun—was made in 1845, in Paris, France. By the late 1870s, cameras for nighttime use had been invented. Soon, these were fitted to many telescopes.

The photographs revolutionized the way astronomers worked. Taking photographs was easier than observing stars by eye and drawing charts by hand, and was often more accurate. Photographs gave astronomers much longer to examine each image of a star in detail, many times if necessary. They could also be published in **star atlases.**

23

The "Great Debate"

In the early 1920s, **astronomers** were caught up in a great debate about the nature of the universe. Some believed that our **galaxy,** the **Milky Way,** was the whole universe. Others believed that the Milky Way was just one part of a much larger universe, containing many other galaxies, **nebulae,** and stars. In 1920, a special scientific meeting was held in Washington, D.C., to discuss this issue. There were two key speakers, with very different opinions: Harlow Shapley, from Mount Wilson, and, his opponent, astronomer H. D. Curtis, from Lick **Observatory** on Mount Hamilton in California.

Harlow Shapley (1885–1972) worked at the Mount Wilson Observatory from 1914 to 1921.

One big galaxy

Shapley argued that our galaxy, the Milky Way, was disk-shaped and 300,000 **light-years** wide, and that spiral nebulae were part of it. He also thought that our sun was in the outer regions of the Milky Way. Shapley had studied groups of stars known as **"globular clusters."** In 1917, he had managed to work out the size of these clusters, and he used this information to suggest a size for the whole Milky Way. At about the same time, his colleague, van Maanen, had been studying spiral-shaped nebulae. He used a series of photos taken several years apart to show that these nebulae were twisting around and around. No one was really sure what this discovery meant, but van Maanen claimed that it proved that the spiral nebulae were very close to Earth.

Putting these two sets of research together, Shapley believed that there could be only one galaxy, and that it must be very large.

Faraway spirals

Curtis claimed that our Milky Way galaxy was only 30,000 light-years wide, and that spiral nebulae were separate galaxies. He thought that the sun lay at the center of the Milky Way. At Lick Observatory, where Curtis worked, astronomer James Keeler also worked on spiral nebulae. But he studied them in a different way. He discovered that there were many millions more spiral nebulae to be seen than anyone had imagined, and that they could be seen everywhere in space. The farther away from Earth he looked, the smaller and fainter the nebulae seemed to be. Curtis could not measure precisely how far away they were, but, by comparing the sizes of different nebulae, he argued that some of them must lie outside the boundaries of the Milky Way.

Today, we know that Shapley and Curtis were both partly right and partly wrong. But in 1920, the world's astronomers had to wait a little longer to settle the argument. Between 1923 and 1925, Edwin Hubble discovered the truth.

The Milky Way was given that name because early astronomers thought that it looked like a stream of milky light across the sky. Today, we know that the Milky Way galaxy is actually spiral-shaped.

LIGHT-YEARS

A light-year is the enormous distance traveled by light in one year—5.9 trillion miles (9.46 trillion kilometers). Light-years are used by astronomers to measure vast distances in space. Light travels very quickly, at about 186,000 miles (300,000 kilometers) per second. Nothing can travel faster than the speed of light.

A Great Discovery

HENRIETTA SWAN LEAVITT

Working from photographs, American **astronomer** Henrietta Swan Leavitt (1868–1921) discovered over 2,400 variable stars. Leavitt had observed something very interesting, and extremely important, about a group of variable stars known as Cepheids. The brightness of Cepheid stars was linked to the time it took for them to change from bright to faint. All stars that changed at the same rate were equally bright, and all stars of equal brightness changed at the same rate. Leavitt's important work helped Hubble to formulate his own theories about the universe.

Henrietta Leavitt worked with lists and photographs of stars.

In 1923, Edwin chose one particular **nebula** to investigate. Almost right away, he discovered that it contained some very interesting variable stars— stars that change from bright to faint, and then back to bright again, in a regular pattern. Some of them were **Cepheids,** the type of variable stars that had been used by Henrietta Leavitt and Harlow Shapley to measure distances across space.

A new observation

Edwin's chosen nebula was called Andromeda. It had been studied by other astronomers for many years, but none of them had observed these Cepheid stars. Even Edwin's critics, including Shapley, agreed that he was a brilliant observer. He was patient and hard-working, had an excellent memory, and paid great attention to even the smallest details. This led him to notice things that other astronomers simply did not see. With the best telescope in the world at Mount Wilson to help him, Edwin was unbeatable.

The answer!

Using Leavitt's and Shapley's findings to help him, Edwin's next step was to work out how far away Andromeda was from Earth. The result—700,000 **light-years** away—surprised him and everyone else. Since Shapley himself had calculated that the whole **Milky Way galaxy** was only 300,000 light-years wide, this meant that Andromeda must be outside it. The "Big Galaxy" theory was wrong—there were many separate nebulae and galaxies within one vast universe. In early 1926, Edwin published his findings, and the world read about the first recognized galaxy outside the Milky Way.

These two images of a Cepheid star in M100 galaxy were taken 22 days apart. They show how the star (in the center of each picture) changes in brightness.

In 1917, Harlow Shapley had used Leavitt's discovery about Cepheids to work out a way of measuring space. Leavitt had claimed that all Cepheids changing at the same rate should appear equally bright to observers on Earth. But Shapley found a group of Cepheids that did not fit this pattern. They all changed at the same rate, but some looked bright and others were faint. Shapley realized this must mean that the bright Cepheids were closer to Earth, while the faint ones were farther away. Using complicated mathematics, Shapley worked out the distance of one Cepheid star from Earth. He then compared its brightness with other Cepheids and calculated how close they were.

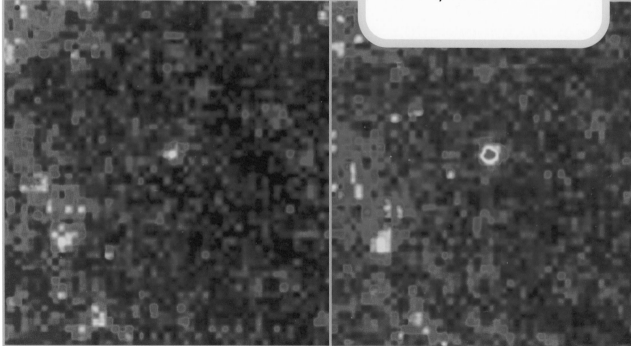

The Expanding Universe

Albert Einstein (sitting, second from left), sometimes considered the world's most famous scientist, visited Mount Wilson Observatory. He met Edwin Hubble (standing, left) and discussed his theories with him.

SPECTROSCOPY

The technique of spectroscopy involves passing rays of light through different gases to form special patterns, or spectra. Each chemical substance has a different spectrum. Astronomers can find out the chemical composition of stars by comparing their spectra with the spectra of known chemicals on Earth.

Hubble's discovery that there were many **galaxies** was soon linked to the other great scientific topic of the 1920s—Einstein's **theory of relativity.** Albert Einstein had put forward the idea that the universe might be expanding. **Astronomers** already had some information that suggested this. As early as 1912, Vesto Slipher used a technique called **spectroscopy** to analyze the light arriving on Earth from distant **nebulae.** He found that light from some of the nebulae was **red-shifted.** This meant that the nebulae were moving away from observers on Earth.

Edwin realized that his own observations could build on Slipher's work, to find out whether Einstein's theory of an expanding universe was true or false.

How fast and how far?

From 1925 on, Edwin devoted his time to working out how fast the nebulae he observed were moving away from Earth, and how far away they had traveled. This was a very complicated task, involving hours of analyzing photographs and **spectra.** Edwin was greatly helped by one of the Mount Wilson assistants, Milton Humason. Edwin worked on photographs while Humason studied spectra. Together, they observed many nebulae and galaxies moving away from Earth.

Milton Humason (1891–1972) was an expert in photographing the spectra of nebulae. Without his help, Edwin's own work would not have progressed so far.

Edwin noticed that the farther away a nebula or galaxy was, the faster it was moving. In other words, the universe was definitely expanding—and it was getting bigger in all directions at once! To help people understand this, Edwin asked them to imagine a balloon, covered with little pictures of nebulae or galaxies. As the balloon is blown up, all the pictures are pushed farther apart.

In 1929, Edwin found a way of describing his findings in mathematical language. This explanation became known as **Hubble's Law,** and has been used by astronomers studying the growth of the universe ever since. He also worked out the **Hubble constant,** a form of mathematical shorthand used in calculations to measure the speed at which nebulae or galaxies move, together with their distance from the person observing them. The Hubble constant is usually represented by an *H.* It is still important in astronomers' calculations today.

The High Life

Edwin Hubble was now a world-famous **astronomer.** When he was not on duty at the Mount Wilson **Observatory,** he and Grace enjoyed a busy social life. They liked giving and attending elegant parties, belonging to exclusive country clubs, and making friends with rich, fashionable people from the United States and Europe. They had a beautiful home in San Marino, California, with oak floors, stained-glass windows, and big log fires. Grace was a charming hostess, and the Hubbles' entertained many top celebrities, including glamorous Hollywood film stars, powerful bankers and politicians, and interesting artists, writers, and thinkers. They also held regular evening suppers and Sunday brunches for scientists at their home. The Hubbles' provided food, and a blackboard where learned guests could draw diagrams and write down calculations.

Edwin and Grace were photographed in the late 1930s. Together, they led a busy, glamorous social life, in Europe as well as in the United States.

Visitors to Europe

Edwin and Grace also loved traveling. During the 1920s and 1930s, there were no cheap air tickets, and long-distance travel by ocean liner was too expensive for most people to afford. But Edwin and Grace had the money to pay for long trips to Europe and went there often.

Edwin's colleagues at Mount Wilson were annoyed that he took so much time off work, but Edwin claimed his visits were to meet European scientists, and to discuss his research with them. On these trips, he did give public lectures, and they were a great success.

He looked impressive and spoke well, unlike many other scientists who were difficult for nonexperts to understand. However, the Hubbles' spent most of their time in Europe visiting theaters, country houses, gardens, and art galleries, and meeting other rich and famous people. Some people thought that Edwin's money made him less successful as an astronomer, since his travels and entertainment kept him away from his work.

Privilege

Grace had been brought up to think that this comfortable, pleasant existence should be her normal way of life, but it was a great change from the plain and simple lifestyle followed by Edwin's own family. It was also enjoyed only by a privileged few at that time. The 1930s were an era of economic depression. The U.S. stock market crashed, many businesses failed, and millions of people became homeless and unemployed.

"In Dr. Hubble's case I find very great difficulty in understanding his attitude toward the organization [Mount Wilson Observatory] which has made his scientific work possible. I do not think it [is] in any way deliberate but results from an extreme form of individualism and personal ambition, together with a type of obtuseness regarding his relations to the Institution and other scientific men.... It has injured him seriously among astronomers...."

From a letter by Walter Adams, director of Mount Wilson Observatory, 1934. (Source: *Edwin Hubble, Mariner of the Nebulae* by Gale E. Christianson)

Unemployed men line up for work in a labor exchange in San Francisco in the 1930s.

Back to War

This is German Nazi leader Adolf Hitler making a speech to his supporters in 1936. Hitler led Germany in the war against England, France, and Russia.

In 1939, another war began in Europe—World War II. As in 1914, it was fought between Britain and France against Germany, with many other nations joining in on both sides. Once again, Edwin was deeply concerned. He did not want to see his European friends and colleagues harmed in any way. At first the United States did not get involved in the war, but after December 7, 1941, when Japanese planes bombed the U.S. fleet anchored at Pearl Harbor in the Pacific Ocean, United States troops joined the fight in support of Britain and its **allies.**

At the proving ground

Being over 50, Edwin was too old to fight, but he was asked by the United States government to help with several secret scientific projects. He replied that he would prefer to serve his country "as a soldier," so he was put in charge of ballistics testing at the U.S. Army's Aberdeen Proving Ground in Maryland. Ballistics is the science of weapons that fire projectiles such as bullets, and the proving ground was a firing range where all newly designed guns were tested before they were issued to soldiers on the battlefield. Testing them was an important, responsible, and sometimes extremely dangerous job.

These bombed U.S. warships are burning in Pearl Harbor in 1941. Japan was an ally of Hitler's Germany during World War II.

By the 1940s, there were many new, "scientific" guns and rockets. They seemed safe in the design laboratory, but were often unpredictable and risky to use.

Edwin enjoyed his work at the proving ground. He felt pleased to be doing what he could to help win the war. In his eagerness, he pushed himself—and the men who worked for him—very hard. But gradually, he won his men's respect. He insisted on test-firing a dangerous new bazooka, or hand-held rocket launcher, himself and repeated the tests until he had found the cause of the problem. He could easily have been killed.

Home in Aberdeen

Women were not normally allowed on firing ranges, but Grace was unwilling to be parted from Edwin for long. She and Edwin lived in a small old cottage that was hot in the summer and freezing in the winter. Grace did her best to turn the hut into a home, and even tamed many of the half-wild cats that roamed the nearby woods so that Edwin would have pets to replace those he had left behind in California.

In Hubble's words:

"This is our war. The final stake is our freedom and the freedom of our children. Let us never forget that this freedom, this liberty, is the heritage of brave men who the world over, since time began, have fought to achieve and maintain it."

Edwin Hubble, in a speech to persuade Americans to join the war. (From *Edwin Hubble, Mariner of the Nebulae* by Gale E. Christianson)

Problems at Home

World War II ended in 1945, and Edwin was delighted that the world was at peace again. However, he was shocked by his country's use of nuclear weapons to force Japan to surrender. The world's first **atom bomb** was dropped on August 6, 1945, on the Japanese city of Hiroshima. Over 150,000 people were killed or injured in a single explosion, and a wide area was polluted by **radioactive** dust. A second atom bomb was dropped on the Japanese city of Nagasaki, only a few days later, on August 9—with similarly disastrous results.

The Japanese city of Hiroshima was devastated after the world's first atom bomb was dropped there in 1945.

Ban the bomb!

Leading physicists had helped the U.S. government to develop nuclear weapons, and many other scientists were impressed by their technical achievement. But Edwin was horrified. He strongly disapproved of all nuclear weapons. He campaigned to ban the bomb, and became a strong supporter of many organizations working for international peace.

A new telescope

Edwin left the Aberdeen Proving Ground in 1946 to return to Mount Wilson. But when he reached the **observatory,** he found that life was far from peaceful there. His stormy relationship with van Maanen continued, and he felt hurt and angry to discover that he was not being considered for an important job overseeing a new observatory, being built at Mount Palomar, not far away. This observatory was to have a huge new telescope, even more powerful than the one at Mount Wilson—and more up-to-date.

The new telescope installed in 1948 at Mount Palomar Observatory replaced the Mount Wilson telescope as the largest in the world. It was twice the size, and could see twice as far into space.

Building this telescope was very costly, and the Mount Wilson team that was planning the new observatory spent long hours in careful discussions with wealthy individuals and charitable organizations to persuade them to pay for it. Edwin had played very little part in these talks, or in planning the new telescope. Although he organized his own research very carefully and kept detailed observation records, he was very bad at day-to-day administration, and was famous for not answering letters—even important ones. But even though Edwin would not have been good at or enjoyed being in charge of the new observatory, he believed that the job should have been offered to him. He was one of America's greatest **astronomers,** after all! But a respected scientist, Ira S. Bowen, who had also done great work on **nebulae** and **spectra,** was chosen instead.

IRA S. BOWEN

Ira S. Bowen was professor of physics at the California Institute of Technology (Caltech) before being made director of Mount Wilson in 1945. He was well known for his work on "nebulium" lines, or lines in the spectra of gaseous nebulae, and had won the Draper Medal, a great U.S. scientific honor.

Seeing Farther into Space

Soon after the new Hale **reflecting telescope** at Mount Palomar was installed in 1948, Edwin was invited to use it. He began early in 1949. Like everyone else, he was amazed by its seeing power. With a mirror measuring 200 inches (5 meters) across, it replaced Mount Wilson's telescope as the largest in the world. Countless millions more stars, **nebulae,** and **galaxies** could be seen from Earth for the first time.

New questions

For Edwin and his colleagues, this "eye on the sky" opened up whole new space frontiers to explore. It also made them wonder what lay beyond these newly-discovered stars. Together with his friend and assistant, Humason, Edwin used the new telescope to continue the research he had started before World War II, measuring how far nebulae and galaxies were from Earth, and how fast they were traveling. Working with two other trusted colleagues, Walter Baade and Allan Sandage, Edwin also used this information to revise his calculations of the **Hubble constant,** and to check the accuracy of some of his earlier findings.

Edwin stands by the "barrel" (long metal tube) housing the huge mirror of the Mount Palomar telescope in 1949. Together, the barrel and mirror weighed 500 tons.

THE BIG BANG

Between 1927 and 1930, scientists such as Georges Lemaître, from France, and Arthur Eddington, from Britain, put forward early versions of the big bang theory. According to this, the universe began about 15 billion years ago, with a massive explosion. Then it started to expand, and has done so ever since. Most astronomers today accept the big bang theory.

Other **astronomers** hoped that Edwin's work at Mount Palomar would help them solve the biggest questions of all, like how old is the universe, when did it begin, and will it ever end? They wanted to use Edwin's measurements of how fast the universe was expanding to calculate how long it had taken to reach its present size, and to work out how big or small it had been to begin with. They hoped to prove the **big bang theory.** They realized that by looking very far out into space, they were also looking back in time. Because the universe is expanding, the farther away a star or galaxy is, the older it is, and the more it might be able to tell us about how the universe began.

THE END OF THE UNIVERSE?

Astronomers have suggested several different ideas about the future of the universe:
• The universe will gradually stop expanding and stay at one size.
• The universe will stop expanding and collapse into a big crunch.
• The universe will collapse, but will start all over again with a new big bang. This is called the bouncing universe theory.
• The universe will go on expanding forever. In 2000, scientists in the U.S. calculated that this is the most likely to happen. But no one can be sure!

The Mount Palomar telescope, seen through the observatory dome, has a massive metal framework supporting its long barrel.

Illness and Disappointment

Before his heart attack, Edwin was rarely seen without his pipe. After he became ill, his doctors banned him from smoking, but he still kept a collection of his favorite pipes in his study, to look at—and sometimes hold between his teeth—as he worked.

When Edwin returned to California from his work at the Aberdeen Proving Ground, everyone noticed that he seemed much older and more tired than before. Grace hoped that her care and California's mild climate would help him recover. But over two years later, when he started work at Mount Palomar, Edwin still did not look well. He was past 50, and had smoked strong pipe tobacco for almost 30 years. Today, we know that all smoking is dangerous to one's health, but this had not been discovered at that time. Also, since his marriage, Edwin had learned to enjoy fine food, which was often a little too rich and not very healthy.

Close to death

After several months' work with the new Mount Palomar telescope, Edwin was tired and decided to take a break. He and Grace went on vacation to a cabin they owned in a wild, remote region of Colorado. Edwin hoped to go fishing, and Grace planned to watch birds and read new books. But a few days after they arrived, Edwin suffered a serious heart attack. He was rushed to the nearest hospital. Four days later, he had another attack and very nearly died. Against all the odds, he survived, but he never fully recovered. He was weak and very tired, and would often fall asleep in the evenings with his cat on his lap. Even so, he went back to work as soon as the doctors allowed. He also made a final trip to Britain, where he gave a very important public lecture, attended by the queen.

Why no prize?

During his brilliant career, Edwin won many prizes. But he had not yet won the Nobel prize—the greatest honor any scientist can hope to achieve. Most of Edwin's colleagues felt that he deserved this prize, but thry could understand why he had not yet been given one. This was partly because there was no separate prize for astronomy, so **astronomers** had to compete with other scientists for honors. New scientific discoveries were being made all the time, and there were too many possible winners to make a fair choice. Edwin's fellow scientists also felt that perhaps his quarrels with his colleagues had made his work less well respected than it deserved to be. But when they learned how sick he was, they began a campaign—strongly supported by Grace—to ask the Nobel committee to consider Edwin for a prize.

Edwin was in a relaxed and happy mood on this fishing trip. He was particularly fond of trout fishing.

After Hubble

Radio telescopes use antennae inside huge dish-shaped receivers to collect radio waves from distant stars as they reach Earth. This telescope is the Lovell Radio Telescope at Jodrell Bank, in Cheshire, England.

Sadly, Edwin Hubble never won his Nobel prize. In 1953, he died, suddenly and peacefully, as Grace drove him home after a busy morning's work. Edwin's ashes were buried in a secret, unmarked grave, without any funeral service or tombstone. This was what he wanted. When Grace died in 1981, she was secretly buried beside him.

However, Hubble's work did not die with him. Since 1953, **astronomers** have continued his quest to measure the universe and to understand it better. They have also used his findings to help investigate some strange predictions made by Einstein's **theory of relativity,** such as whether the universe is curved or flat. By 2000, most scientists have agreed that it is flat and dish-shaped.

ONGOING IMPACT Visible and invisible

Human eyes can see only a small amount of the light that arrives on Earth from space. So today, astronomers use radio telescopes and other machines to discover and collect all the other unseen rays given off by stars, **galaxies,** and **nebulae.** Even with technology improving all the time, today's scientists still rely on Hubble's discoveries to interpret what they see.

Astronomers still use huge telescopes, like the ones Edwin used in California, but they have developed exciting new ways of observing and recording the stars. One of their most important techniques is **radio astronomy,** a way of detecting objects in space that cannot be seen by human eyes. Astronomers also measure and record invisible **microwaves** produced soon after the **big bang,** almost 15 billion years ago. The existence of these microwaves was first suggested in 1946 by American scientist George Gamow. But they were not detected until 1965, when radio astronomers monitoring the first communications satellite orbiting, or circling, the earth accidentally picked up faint microwave signals. Then, they helped prove that the "Big Bang" theory was probably true. Today, astronomers use this "background radiation" to find out more about what the universe was like billions of years ago.

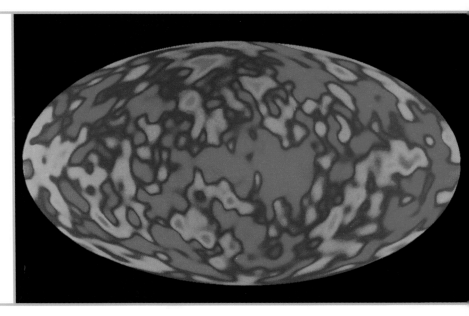

This photo, taken by the Cosmic Background Explorer spacecraft in 1993, shows variations in the temperature of the background radiation. It helped to convince many scientists that the "Big Bang" theory was correct.

Hubble's Memorial

Today, Hubble's name has become well known to many people who are not scientists or **astronomers.** The Hubble Space Telescope (HST), named in his honor, regularly sends dramatic new pictures of the distant regions of space back to Earth.

The primary mirror of the Hubble Telescope measures 8.5 feet (2.5 meters) in diameter.

A telescope in space

A telescope was first sent beyond the earth's atmosphere in 1962, on board the American Orbiting Solar **Observatory** I. It marked a major breakthrough in space exploration. When Hubble was alive, all astronomers used Earth-based telescopes. Even when these telescopes were on mountaintops, clouds and atmospheric pollution sometimes hid the stars from view. Space telescopes were designed to overcome this problem by orbiting the earth high above the atmosphere. They collected light rays or radio waves without any interference from pollution or the weather, and sent the information back to Earth.

"The Hubble Space Telescope may yet help astronomers 'unlock a secret of the universe.'"

(Astronomer Trinh Xuan Thuan, in *The Changing Universe, Big Bang and After*)

The HST was built in the United States, but it contains telescopes and other instruments designed and made by scientists from all over the world. It was launched in 1990, and is the first in a planned series of Great Observatories, all of which should greatly increase our knowledge of the universe. The HST contains five major instruments for making observations: two cameras, two machines for recording **spectra,** and a sensitive device for measuring faint rays of light.

"*While Columbus sailed three thousand miles and discovered one continent and some islands, Hubble has roamed through infinite space and discovered hundreds of new worlds, islands, sub-continents and constellations not just a few thousand miles away, but trillions of miles out yonder.*"

(From *Travel Magazine,* September 1949)

The Hubble Space Telescope is launched from the space shuttle.

The HST ran into serious problems soon after its launch because the mirror in its main telescope was faulty, but it was still able to send dramatic pictures of the planets Pluto and Saturn back to Earth. In 1993, the telescope was repaired, and a new camera was installed by astronauts from the U.S. space shuttle. This has allowed the HST to continue with its most important task, observing distant **galaxies** to help astronomers work out a new, more accurate value for the **Hubble constant**—and to show whether the universe is still expanding at the same rate.

Hubble had access to some of the most up-to-date equipment of his day. Using his brilliant observational skills, he was able to see what other astronomers had missed, and show us how the universe works. Today, the HST continues to send valuable data back to Earth from space. This new information, and the excellent quality of the HST photos, would doubtless have pleased and excited Hubble. Who knows what new discoveries he might have made if he had been able to see them?

Timeline

1889	Edwin Powell Hubble is born in Marshfield, Missouri.
1897	Yerkes **Observatory** is built at Williams Bay, Wisconsin.
1901	The Hubble family moves to Wheaton, Illinois.
1904	Mount Wilson Observatory is built at Pasadena, California.
1906	Hubble wins a **scholarship** to the University of Chicago. Becomes a successful heavyweight boxer.
1910	Hubble wins a prestigious Rhodes scholarship to study at Oxford University in England.
1912	Henrietta Swan Leavitt's study of **Cepheid** stars provides a way of measuring how far Cepheids are away from Earth. Vesto Slipher notices that **nebulae** are moving; observes **red shifts** in the **spectra** of **galaxies.**
1913	Hubble's father dies. Hubble returns home from Oxford.
1913–14	Hubble spends a year in his family home, helping his mother. He teaches high school and works as a legal clerk.
1914	Hubble joins staff at Yerkes Observatory and begins research into nebulae.
1914–18	First World War. The United States enters the war in 1917.
1915	Albert Einstein publishes General **Theory of Relativity.**
1917	Hubble volunteers to join the U.S. Army. Hubble earns a Ph.D. from the University of Chicago. Harlow Shapley shows that the sun is not at the center of the **Milky Way** galaxy. Telescope built at Mount Wilson Observatory. It is the largest in the world.
1918	Hubble goes to Europe to fight in the war.
1919	Hubble joins the staff of Mount Wilson Observatory.
1920	Hubble meets Grace Burke.
1923	Hubble proves that the universe contains many separate galaxies.
1924	Hubble marries Grace Burke.
1925	Hubble works out a classification scheme for galaxies.
1927	Georges Lemaître is the first **astronomer** to suggest the **big bang theory** of the origins of the universe.
1929	Hubble discovers the **Hubble constant** (a mathematical term used in calculations) and **Hubble's Law,** that the more distant a galaxy is, the faster it is traveling away from the earth. This shows that the universe is expanding.

1930–40	Hubble becomes very famous in Europe as well as in the United States. He travels widely and gives public lectures.
1937	First radio telescope built.
1939–45	Second World War.
1940	Hubble urges U.S. government to help defend Britain. The U.S. joins in war in 1941.
1942	Hubble appointed head of ballistics at the U.S. Army's Aberdeen Proving Ground in Maryland. Grace joins him later.
1945	Hubble returns to Mount Wilson Observatory.
1946	Hubble begins campaigning against nuclear weapons.
1948	Hale **reflecting telescope** is dedicated at Mount Palomar, California.
1949	Hubble begins work at Mount Palomar. Has two near-fatal heart attacks.
1953	Edwin Hubble dies at age 63.
1990	The Hubble Space Telescope is launched.

More Books to Read

Cole, Michael D. *Hubble Space Telescope: Exploring the Universe.* Berkeley Heights, N.J.: Enslow Publishers, 1999.

Datnow, Claire. *Edwin Hubble: Discoverer of Galaxies.* Berkeley Heights, N.J.: Enslow Publishers, 1997.

Fox, Mary V. *Edwin Hubble: American Astronomer.* Danbury, Conn.: Franklin Watts, Inc.: 1997

Glossary

ally country that has agreed to be friendly toward others

astronomer someone who studies space

astronomy study of space and all that it contains, such as stars and planets

atom bomb bomb that creates a massive explosion by splitting the nuclei, or central parts, of atoms (tiny particles that make up all matter)

big bang theory description of the origins of the universe, accepted by most astronomers today. According to this theory, the universe began about 15 billion years ago with a massive explosion, and has continued expanding ever since.

Cepheid type of variable star that changes from bright to faint at a regular interval

galaxy collection of stars held together by gravity

globular cluster globe-shaped collection of stars. Each globular cluster can contain hundreds of thousands of stars.

gravity natural force that attracts objects to one another. The larger the mass of an object, the greater its power to attract.

Hubble constant special kind of number, used as mathematical shorthand, that describes two things: the speed at which galaxies move through space, and how far they are from observers on Earth

Hubble's Law scientific fact about galaxies, discovered by Hubble, that the faster they are moving away from observers on Earth, the farther away they are

light-year distance light travels in one year, or about 5.9 trillion miles (about 9.46 trillion kilometers)

microwave form of radiation that cannot by seen by the human eye

Milky Way spiral galaxy that contains our solar system

nebula mysterious, cloudy formation in space. There are four different kinds of nebulae: clusters of stars; shells of gas surrounding decaying stars; clouds of space dust and gas; and very distant galaxies.

observatory building where astronomers use telescopes to study space

philosophy study of the history of ideas leading to the creation of new ideas about truth and knowledge

radioactive giving off dangerous radiation. Some kinds of radiation can kill.

radio astronomy studying the universe by using telescopes that collect invisible rays given off by stars and other objects in space

red-shifted giving off more red light than expected, a sign that an object is moving away from the person observing it. This is because light waves are more spread out, and appear redder, as an object becomes more distant.

reflecting telescope telescope that works by collecting rays of light given off by stars and other objects in space and reflecting them with mirrors to produce a magnified image

scholarship prize of money or other aid given to a student

spectroscopy way of measuring the chemical composition of objects, including stars, by passing the rays of light they give off through special gases

spectrum pattern formed by light rays as they are passed through gases during the process of spectroscopy. Astronomers study the spectra of stars to find out what they are made of.

star atlas collection of maps, charts, and photographs showing the sky at night, that may include all the known stars and other objects in space

theory of relativity two scientific laws formulated by Albert Einstein in 1905 (special relativity) and 1915 (general relativity). Special relativity states that the speed at which an object travels can only be measured in relation to the person observing it. Things will not appear the same to an observer who is moving as they would to an observer who is standing still. General relativity states that space and time are changed, or curved, by the presence of any mass. The more massive an object, the more space and time become curved. Astronomers use these theories to help them understand what they see when they look into space.

Index

American Civil War 6
American Orbiting Solar
    Observatory 1 42
Andromeda nebula 15, 26–27
arrays 41
astronomers 4, 5, 8, 10–11, 13,
    41, 42–43
    HST 42–43
    atom bomb 34

Baade, Walter 36
background radiation 41
ballistics 32
"Big Bang" 36, 37, 41
"Big Crunch" 37
"bouncing universe" 37
Bowen, Ira S. 35

Cannon, Annie Jump 19
Cepheids 26–27
Curtis, H. D. 24, 25

debates 24–25

Einstein, Albert 28–29, 40
Elizabeth II, Queen 39
expanding universe 5, 28–29,
    36–37, 39

galaxies 4–5, 15, 24–25, 27,
    28–29, 36, 40, 43
Gamow, George 41
globular clusters 24
gravity 4

Hale reflecting telescope 36
Harvard College Observatory
    19
Hubble, Edwin
    army life 16–17, 32–33
    astronomy 14–15, 18, 20,
        22–23, 25, 34–37
    discoveries 26–29, 40
    early life 6–13

Hubble, Edwin (continued)
    illness 38–39
    quarrels 34, 39
    social life 30–31
    space telescope 5, 42–43
Hubble, Grace 20–21, 30–31,
    33, 35, 38–40
Hubble, John 6, 8, 9, 12
Hubble, Lucy 16
Hubble Space Telescope
    (HST) 5, 42–43
Hubble, Virginia 6, 8, 12, 13
Hubble, William 12–13
Hubble constant 5, 29, 36,
    43
Hubble's Law 29
Humason, Milton 29, 36

Jansky, Karl 41

Keeler, James 8, 10, 25

Leavitt, Henrietta 19, 26, 27
Lick Observatory 10, 24, 25
light-years 15, 22, 24, 25, 27
Lowell Observatory 10, 15

microwaves 41
Milky Way 4, 24–25, 27
Mount Palomar Observatory
    34–38
Mount Wilson Observatory 4,
    15

nebulae 4–5, 8, 10
    expanding universe 28–29,
        36, 40
    observations 15, 22, 24–29
Nobel prize 39, 40
nuclear weapons 34

observatories 4, 9–10, 14–15
    Great 42
    Mount Wilson 18–19, 24,
        26, 29, 30, 34, 35
    orbits 41, 42

philosophy 9
photographs 22–23, 26, 29

radioactivity 34
radio astronomy 41
radio telescopes 40–41
Reber, Grote 41
red shift 28
relativity theory 28, 40
Rhodes scholarship 10

Sandage, Allan 36
satellites 41
Shapley, Harlow 10, 23–27
skyscrapers 7
Slipher, Vesto 10, 15, 28–29
space shuttle 43
spectra 28–29, 35, 42
spectroscopy 28
star atlases 15, 23

telescopes 7, 9, 14–15, 17
    HST 5, 42–43
    Mount Palomar 34–38
    Mount Wilson 18–19, 22,
        26
    photography 23
    radio 40–41

University of Chicago 9,
    13–14
University of Oxford 10–13,
    16

van Maanen, Adriaan 23, 24,
    34
variable stars 26
Very Large Array (VLA) 41

World War I 16–17
World War II 32–34, 36

Yerkes Observatory 14–16